# DISCOVERING SHARKS AND RAYS

by Charis Mather

Fusion Books, an imprint of Bearport Publishing by FlutterBee

**Credits**
All images are courtesy of Shutterstock.com, unless otherwise stated. Recurring – Net Vector, Baskiabat, NotionPic, PCH.Vector, Susann Guenther, LAtelier. Cover – Andrea Izzotti, Jsegalexplore, nicolasvoisin44. 2–3 – Jsegalexplore.4–5 – MVshop, satit sewtiw. 6–7 – Martin Prochazkacz, Michelle de Villiers. 8–9 – le bouil baptiste, Thierry Eidenweil, frantisekhojdysz. 10–11 – JuanxoGonzalez, Photos by Tropiclens. 12–13 – Martin Prochazkacz. 14–15 – Jesus Cobaleda. 16–17 – Alex Rush, Jan Philip Morton. 18–19 – Chaos2Light Images, Nick Fox. 22–23 – Serena Kelly, ShutterBumpkin.

**Bearport Publishing Company Product Development Team**
Kayla Eggert, Theresa Emminizer, Kim Jones, Allison Juda, Cole Nelson, Naomi Reich, Steve Scheluchin, Tiana Tran

Library of Congress Cataloging-in-Publication Data is available at www.loc.gov or upon request from the publisher.

ISBN: 979-8-89577-815-9 (hardcover)
ISBN: 979-8-89577-827-2 (ebook)



For more information, write to Bearport Publishing, 3500 American Blvd W, Suite 150, Bloomington, MN 55431.
Printed in the United States of America.

# CONTENTS

# ALL ABOARD!

Ahoy there! You are just in time for the See-Gulls Ocean Tour. I am Captain Gulliver, and this is my **crew**. Climb aboard!

CAPTAIN GULLIVER

Earth's oceans are filled with many strange and wonderful creatures. Today, we will be searching for sharks and rays!
Let's set sail!
Aye aye, Captain!
SEE-GULLS
OCEAN TOURS

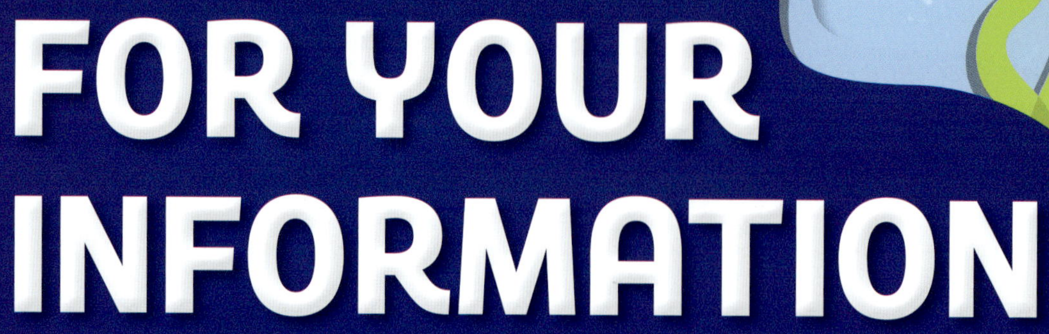

# FOR YOUR INFORMATION

Sharks and rays are types of fish. They have soft skeletons, which helps them move quickly through the water. This also makes them different from most other fish.

Sharks and rays are powerful predators, but they are not all as scary as you might think. Most sharks and rays won't hurt people. They only attack people if they feel **threatened**.

# TIGER SHARKS

You can see how this shark got is name! The markings on the tiger shark's body look similar to a tiger's stripes.

Young tiger sharks have darker stripes than older tiger sharks.

The tiger shark also hunts a bit like a tiger. It moves slowly until it is ready to strike. Then, it speeds toward its **prey**, snapping up the meal with its sharp teeth!

# SPOTTED EAGLE RAYS

Spotted eagle rays have long, whiplike tails with **venomous** stingers at the end. They use their tails to protect themselves from predators.

TAIL

Be careful! A sting from one of these rays can really hurt.

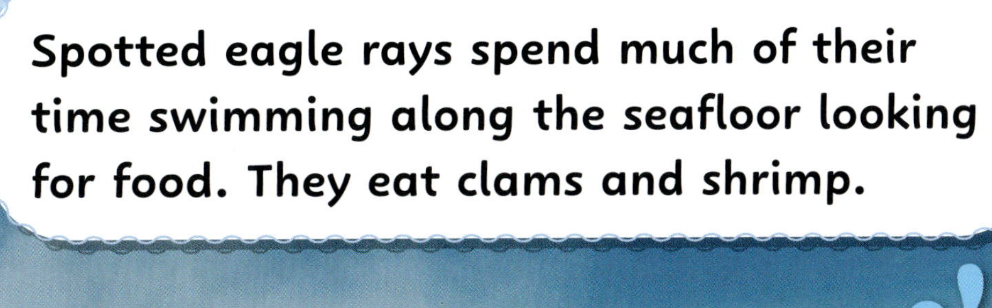

Spotted eagle rays spend much of their time swimming along the seafloor looking for food. They eat clams and shrimp.

Spotted eagle rays can be up to 9 feet (3 m) wide and 8 ft. (2 m) long.

# BASKING SHARKS

Basking sharks are the second-biggest fish in the ocean. Only whale sharks are bigger. And while they might look big and scary, basking sharks are not dangerous.

Basking sharks grow up to 40 ft. (12 m) long.

These sharks are filter feeders that eat tiny creatures called zooplankton. Basking sharks open their mouths wide and get a mouthful of zooplankton-filled water. Then, they push out the water through their gills and swallow the food.
Look! I'm a basking shark!
You need to brush your beak.

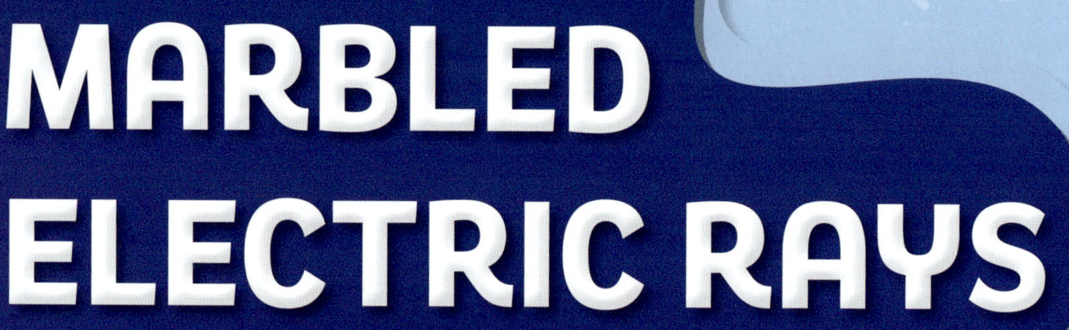

# MARBLED ELECTRIC RAYS

The marbled electric ray is good at hiding. The patterns on its back help it blend in with the ocean floor.

Marbled electric rays shock their prey with **electricity!** Then, they swallow their meal whole.

Marbled electric rays often bury themselves in sand.

# HAMMERHEAD SHARKS

Hammerhead sharks are named for the shapes of their heads. Their eyes are very far apart. This gives the sharks a wide view of the ocean around them.

Hammerheads use special organs called **ampullae** to find prey. Ampullae sense the **electrical fields** of other animals, which helps the shark find its next meal.

Hammerheads hunt for stingrays, squid, and octopuses.

# SAWFISH

The sawfish is another type of ray. And its namesake long snout is not just for show. This body part, called a rostrum, has sharp pieces along the edges called rostral teeth. The rostrum can be used to slash prey into pieces.

ROSTRAL TEETH

Sawfish can grow new rostral teeth to replace ones that are worn down or lost.

The rostrum is also covered in ampullae. When the sawfish senses prey under the sand, it uses its long snout to dig them out.
Thankfully, sawfish mostly eat fish, not birds!

# THRESHER SHARKS

Like most sharks, thresher sharks have lots of sharp teeth. However, their tails are their biggest weapon. When hunting, thresher sharks whip their long tails toward their prey to try and smack them.

Thresher sharks are very fast swimmers, reaching speeds up to 45 miles per hour (72 kph).

Just one strike from a thresher shark's tail can **stun** many fish. Then, the shark uses its teeth to snap up its prey.

Seeing sharks and rays up close is certainly interesting, but I'm glad to head back to land!

There are lots of other amazing animals to see in the ocean. We hope you join us for another See-Gulls Ocean Tour soon!

# GLOSSARY

**ampullae** special organs that can sense electrical fields

**crew** the group of people who work on a ship

**electrical fields** areas in which electric energy is found, such as around animals

**electricity** a type of energy that can cause a painful shock

**organs** parts of living things that have specific, important uses

**prey** animals that are hunted by other animals for food

**stun** to knock out or make dizzy

**threatened** having the feeling of being in danger

**venomous** able to poison another animal through a bite, sting, or scratch

# INDEX